TRICK BISCUITS

Contents

Welcome to *Rigby Navigator* 2

Renewed Framework Teaching Objectives 3

How to use the *Rigby Navigator Plays* Teaching Guides 4

About the Play 6

Lesson 1 8

Lesson 2 9

Focus on (Lesson 1) 10

Focus on (Lesson 2) 11

PCM 1 12

PCM 2 13

Now Stage the Play 14

Welcome to Rigby Navigator

Giving you the Right Tools for the Job
Rigby Navigator is an easy-to-use, versatile programme specially designed to help you unlock the potential of guided reading. It has been developed to make guided reading easy to manage and enjoyable for both teachers and children. The programme provides a compact series of books for fiction, non-fiction, poetry and plays for 7–11 year olds. *Rigby Navigator* also has the flexibility to be used alongside your existing guided reading resources.

Navigator Plays

Rigby Navigator plays have been written to help you deliver creative and effective guided reading sessions for all your pupils. The plays are tailor-made for guided reading lessons, so they provide just the right amount of material and at the right interest level. There are 12 plays, three for each of year groups 3–6 (P4–7), with parts for six characters in each play. These specially written resources make classroom management easy, while giving the children the pleasure of reading complete plays.

Each play is supported by its own Teaching Guide, offering guided reading notes that provide a model for teaching. They put a wealth of ideas at your fingertips for engaging children in the reading of plays and, additionally, include notes on performing the play. The ideas may, of course, be adapted according to the needs of guided reading within your class.

A New Generation of Teacher Support
Each Teaching Guide provides two guided reading lessons. The Guides contain details on how to introduce the plays, questions to ask before, during and after reading, and suggestions for follow-up and independent work. The literacy objectives for each lesson are clearly highlighted.

Appropriate question prompts are given to encourage discussion of, for example, characterisation, setting, theme, format and the differences between prose and play script. Coverage of the Renewed Framework core learning objectives allows children to progress to the higher order reading skills of deductive, inferential and evaluative comprehension, which are essential for SATs preparation.

Differentiation
The wide range of ability levels in the classroom adds to the time needed to prepare for effective guided reading. *Rigby Navigator Plays* Teaching Guides offer teachers flexible routes through the plays so that each guided reading lesson can be differentiated. The plays have been written in sets of three around topics pertinent to each year group. Each set of plays offers a gradient of challenge in order to cater for the range within each class. *Rigby Navigator* Teaching Guides state the National Curriculum Level of each play so that guided reading lessons can be successfully differentiated.

It should be noted that reading play scripts offers some particular challenges. Children may be unfamiliar with the layout of plays in general. They will need to read the stage directions silently and interpret them in line with the text. Some plays use unfamiliar vocabulary in terms of idiom or historical setting. The need for expression, characterisation and interplay with the audience adds another dimension to the reading of these plays. For this reason, the level of the play scripts is somewhat lower than the level of straightforward fiction or non-fiction texts for a particular year group.

Children need to participate in a first run-through to familiarise themselves with the story line. The teacher will guide their interpretation and offer assistance in understanding the context for each play. The children should then have the opportunity to rehearse their own roles and then return to a collaborative re-reading and possibly play-reading performance.

Top Children's Playwrights
Rigby Navigator Plays contains well-crafted plays by respected children's writers, which will capture children's imaginations and develop them as enthusiastic readers and writers of plays.

Narrative Genre Coverage
The *Rigby Navigator* plays in each year group are linked by genre. The genre relates to one or more of the literacy units for that year:
- **Year 3:** Stories with familiar settings; Dialogue and plays
- **Year 4:** Stories with historical settings; Plays
- **Year 5:** Traditional stories, fables, myths, legends; Dramatic conventions
- **Year 6:** Fiction genres.

Models for Writing

The plays also serve as perfect exemplars for children's own writing. The Teaching Guides have a strong focus on writing, drawing on the essential link between reading and writing.

Rigby Navigator Plays and Assessment

Valuable information can be accrued during guided reading about children's application of essential reading skills and strategies. The Teaching Guides include questioning prompts to track children's level of understanding of the teaching objectives of the lesson. This will ensure that you have a clear picture of each child's progress.

Drama and Speaking & Listening

The *Rigby Navigator* plays present significant opportunities for reinforcing and extending children's developing drama, and speaking and listening skills. These include:

- preparing plays for performance or reading aloud, identifying appropriate expression, tone and volume
- developing and using specific vocabulary related to plays (e.g. role, play script, stage directions, rehearsal, performance, prop, sound effects)
- when performing or reading aloud in role, listening carefully to others in order to come in on cue and maintain the pace
- using talk to organise roles and action
- using the language of possibility to investigate and reflect on feelings, behaviour or relationships
- presenting dialogue to engage the interest of an audience
- using drama strategies to explore the plays (e.g. hot-seating to focus on character; freeze-framing to identify significant events)
- identifying and discussing qualities of others' performances.

In addition to the opportunities offered within the lessons themselves, each Teaching Guide contains a double-page spread of guidance for staging and performing the play.

Renewed Framework Teaching Objectives

Tricky Biscuits – Familiar Settings

Lesson 1	Lesson 2
Focus on Features of Play Scripts	**Focus on Reading Aloud with Expression**
Y3 Strand 1: 4 Develop and use specific vocabulary (e.g. play-related words and phrases)	**Y3 Strand 1: 1** Choose and prepare poems or stories [plays] for performance, identifying appropriate expression, tone, volume and use of voices and other sounds
Y3 Strand 7: 1 Identify the main points of sections of text	
Y3 Strand 7: 2 Infer characters' feelings in fiction and consequences in logical explanations	**Y3 Strand 4: 2** Use some drama strategies to explore stories or issues
Y3 Strand 7: 3 Identify how different texts are organised (e.g. recognise the key differences between prose and play script)	**Y3 Strand 7: 1** Identify the main points of sections of text
Y3 Strand 8: 2 Empathise with characters	**Y3 Strand 7: 2** Infer characters' feelings in fiction and consequences in logical explanations
	Y3 Strand 8: 1 Share and compare reasons for reading preferences
	Y3 Strand 9: 1 Make decisions about form and purpose

NOTE: The strand numbers identified in the table above refer to the Renewed Framework core learning strands. They are: **Strand 1:** Speaking; **Strand 4:** Drama; **Strand 7:** Understanding and interpreting texts; **Strand 8:** Engaging with and responding to texts; **Strand 9:** Creating and shaping texts.

How to use the Navigator Plays Teaching Guides

The *Navigator* Teaching Guides offer flexible routes through the plays for guided reading. The Guides put you in control of guided reading, as you choose the routes through the material depending on the needs of your group.

Lesson 1

At a Glance
This section gives you planning support, designed to save you valuable time, by giving you an overview of the play as well as highlighting the literacy opportunities in the text.

Think
This section introduces the play to the children, familiarising them with the features and context of the play script and activating any prior knowledge and experience that they bring to the reading. It may involve talking about the way plays are set out and read, explaining difficult vocabulary or giving an overview of the content. Depending on a group's ability, some children may be able to read the play ahead of the guided reading session.

Read and Respond
In this section of the lesson, the children can predict, reflect, recall, interpret, challenge and respond to the text.

- **Question Prompts:** These questions enable the teacher to assess whether the children have understood the play. If the children have read it in advance, it is a good opportunity for them to recall the story of the play and to retrieve detail.

- **Going Deeper:** This section leads the children deeper into the text, giving them reading strategies to help them understand and interpret it. The children are encouraged to support their views with evidence from the text.

- **Focus on:** This section of the lesson focuses on a number of pages in the play and fulfils a key objective. Children re-read a portion of the play and are encouraged to use specific reading strategies while investigating the text. Often, this focused questioning requires children to read between and beyond the lines of the text.

Reflect
Now the children reflect in detail on the play they have read. This is also an opportunity to consolidate the strategies used.

Follow-up
The PCM for Lesson 1 focuses on response to the text to extend and assess reading comprehension.

Challenge: Differentiation
The main stem of the lesson is the same for all children. You can choose from the range of literacy activities available – from simple recall of fact to more probing and interpretive discussion – according to the group you are taking.

As a guided reading lesson progresses faster with more able children, the Challenge sections extend the main stem of the lesson and build on the teaching that has gone before.

Lesson 2

The second guided reading lesson works in the same way as Lesson 1, but may have different learning objectives and also includes a key writing objective. The follow-up work has a writing focus, and further writing suggestions are also given.

Annotations (callouts)

- Introduces the play and activates children's prior knowledge
- A focused look at the text
- Allows teachers to check comprehension and facilitate group discussion
- Gives an overview of the play and highlights literacy opportunities – saving you time
- Encourages critical thinking
- Consolidates strategies used
- Strong link to writing in Lesson 2 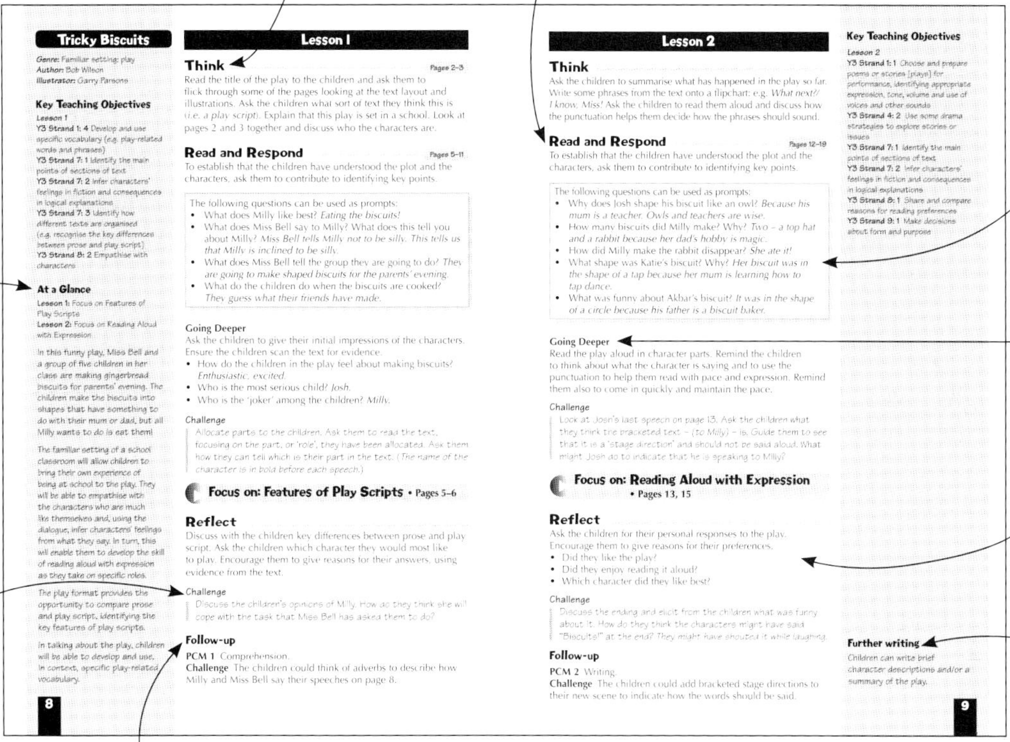
- Differentiated routes through the material put you in control
- Focused follow-up ideas
- Focused question prompts
- Focus section for both lessons
- Annotated pages put you in control
- Challenge sections allow more able children to go even deeper into the text
- One reading and one writing copymaster for each play

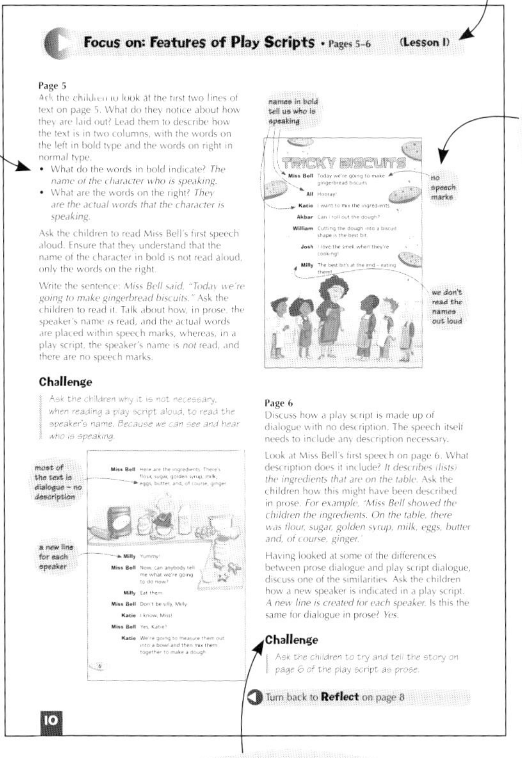

Page 8 — Tricky Biscuits

Genre: Familiar setting: play
Author: Bob Wilson
Illustrator: Garry Parsons

Key Teaching Objectives

Lesson 1
Y3 Strand 1: 4 Develop and use specific vocabulary (e.g. play-related words and phrases)
Y3 Strand 7: 1 Identify the main points of sections of text
Y3 Strand 7: 2 Infer characters' feelings in fiction and consequences in logical explanations
Y3 Strand 7: 3 Identify how different texts are organised (e.g. recognise the key differences between prose and play script)
Y3 Strand 8: 2 Empathise with characters

At a Glance

Lesson 1: Focus on Features of Play Scripts
Lesson 2: Focus on Reading Aloud with Expression

In this funny play, Miss Bell and a group of five children in her class are making gingerbread biscuits for parents' evening. The children make the biscuits into shapes that have something to do with their mum or dad, but all Milly wants to do is eat them!

The familiar setting of a school classroom will allow children to bring their own experience of being at school to the play. They will be able to empathise with the characters who are much like themselves and, using the dialogue, infer characters' feelings from what they say. In turn, this will enable them to develop the skill of reading aloud with expression as they take on specific roles.

The play format provides the opportunity to compare prose and play scripts, identifying the key features of play scripts.

In talking about the play, children will be able to develop and use, in context, specific play-related vocabulary.

Lesson 1

Think
Pages 2–3
Read the title of the play to the children and ask them to flick through some of the pages looking at the text layout and illustrations. Ask the children what sort of text they think this is (i.e. a play script). Explain that this play is set in a school. Look at pages 2 and 3 together and discuss who the characters are.

Read and Respond
Pages 5–11
To establish that the children have understood the plot and the characters, ask them to contribute to identifying key points.

The following questions can be used as prompts:
- What does Milly like best? *Eating the biscuits!*
- What does Miss Bell say to Milly? What does this tell you about Milly? *Miss Bell tells Milly not to be silly. This tells us that Milly is inclined to be silly.*
- What does Miss Bell tell the group they are going to do? *They are going to make shaped biscuits for the parents' evening.*
- What do the children do when the biscuits are cooked? *They guess what their friends have made.*

Going Deeper
Ask the children to give their initial impressions of the characters. Ensure the children scan the text for evidence.
- How do the children in the play feel about making biscuits? *Enthusiastic, excited.*
- Who is the most serious child? *Josh.*
- Who is the 'joker' among the children? *Milly.*

Challenge
Allocate parts to the children. Ask them to read the text, focusing on the part, or 'role', they have been allocated. Ask how they can tell which is their part in the text. *(The name of the character is in bold before each speech.)*

Focus on: Features of Play Scripts • Pages 5–6

Reflect
Discuss with the children key differences between prose and play script. Ask the children which character they would most like to play. Encourage them to give reasons for their answers, using evidence from the text.

Challenge
Discuss the children's opinions of Milly. How do they think she will cope with the task that Miss Bell has asked them to do?

Follow-up
PCM 1 Comprehension
Challenge The children could think of adverbs to describe how Milly and Miss Bell say their speeches on page 8.

Page 9 — Lesson 2

Think
Ask the children to summarise what has happened in the play so far. Write some phrases from the text onto a flipchart: e.g. *What next!! I know, Miss!* Ask the children to read them aloud and discuss how the punctuation helps them decide how the phrases should sound.

Read and Respond
Pages 12–19
To establish that the children have understood the plot and the characters, ask them to contribute to identifying key points.

The following questions can be used as prompts:
- Why does Josh shape his biscuit like an owl? *Because his mum is a teacher. Owls and teachers are wise.*
- How many biscuits did Milly make? Why? *Two – a top hat and a rabbit because her dad's hobby is magic.*
- How did Milly make the rabbit disappear? *She ate it!*
- What shape was Katie's biscuit? Why? *Her biscuit was in the shape of a tap because her mum is learning how to tap dance.*
- What was funny about Akbar's biscuit? *It was in the shape of a circle because his father is a biscuit baker.*

Going Deeper
Read the play aloud in character parts. Remind the children to think about what the character is saying and to use the punctuation to help them read with pace and expression. Remind them also to come in quickly and maintain the pace.

Challenge
Look at Josh's last speech on page 13. Ask the children what they think the bracketed text – *(to Milly)* – is. Guide them to see that it is a 'stage direction' and should not be said aloud. What might Josh do to indicate that he is speaking to Milly?

Focus on: Reading Aloud with Expression • Pages 13, 15

Reflect
Ask the children for their personal responses to the play. Encourage them to give reasons for their preferences.
- Did they like the play?
- Did they enjoy reading it aloud?
- Which character did they like best?

Challenge
Discuss the ending and elicit from the children what was funny about it. How do they think the characters might have said 'Biscuits!' at the end? *They might have shouted it while laughing.*

Follow-up
PCM 2 Writing
Challenge The children could add bracketed stage directions to their new scene to indicate how the words should be said.

Further writing
Children can write brief character descriptions and/or a summary of the play.

Key Teaching Objectives

Lesson 2
Y3 Strand 1: 1 Choose and prepare poems or stories [plays] for performance, identifying appropriate expression, tone, volume and use of voices and other sounds
Y3 Strand 4: 2 Use drama strategies to explore stories or issues
Y3 Strand 7: 1 Identify the main points of sections of text
Y3 Strand 7: 2 Infer characters' feelings in fiction and consequences in logical explanations
Y3 Strand 8: 1 Share and compare reasons for reading preferences
Y3 Strand 9: 1 Make decisions about form and purpose

Page 10 — Focus on: Features of Play Scripts • Pages 5–6 (Lesson 1)

Page 5
Ask the children to look at the first two lines of text on page 5. What do they notice about how they are laid out? Lead them to describe how the text is in two columns, with the words on the left in bold type and the words on right in normal type.
- What do the words in bold indicate? *The name of the character who is speaking.*
- What are the words on the right? *They are the actual words that the character is speaking.*

Ask the children to read Miss Bell's first speech aloud. Ensure that they understand that the name of the character in bold is not read aloud, only the words on the right.

Write the sentence: *Miss Bell said, "Today we're going to make gingerbread biscuits."* Ask the children to read it. Talk about how, in prose, the speaker's name is read, and the actual words are placed within speech marks, whereas, in a play script, the speaker's name is *not* read, and there are no speech marks.

Challenge
Ask the children why it is not necessary, when reading a play script aloud, to read the speaker's name. *Because we can see and hear who is speaking.*

Annotations on sample page:
- names in bold tell us who is speaking
- no speech marks
- we don't read the names out loud
- most of the text is dialogue – no description
- a new line for each speaker

Page 6
Discuss how a play script is made up of dialogue with no description. The speech itself needs to include any description necessary.

Look at Miss Bell's first speech on page 6. What description does it include? *It describes (lists) the ingredients that are on the table.* Ask the children how this might have been described in prose. For example, *Miss Bell showed the children the ingredients. On the table, there was flour, sugar, golden syrup, milk, eggs, butter and, of course, ginger.*

Having looked at some of the differences between prose dialogue and play script dialogue, discuss some of the similarities. Ask the children how a new speaker is indicated in a play script. *A new line is created for each speaker.* Is this the same for dialogue in prose? *Yes.*

Challenge
Ask the children to try and tell the story on page 6 of the play script as prose.

◀ Turn back to **Reflect** on page 8

PCM 1 — Tricky Biscuits

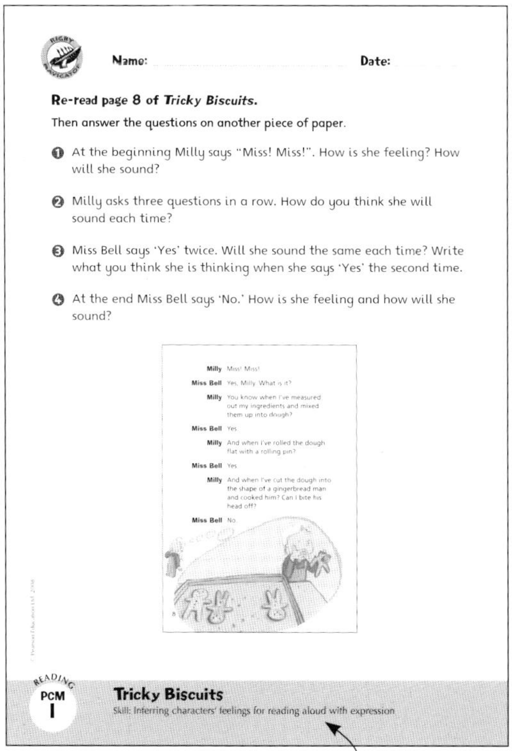

Name: _____ **Date:** _____

Re-read page 8 of *Tricky Biscuits*.

Then answer the questions on another piece of paper.

1. At the beginning Milly says "Miss! Miss!". How is she feeling? How will she sound?

2. Milly asks three questions in a row. How do you think she will sound each time?

3. Miss Bell says 'Yes' twice. Will she sound the same each time? Write what you think she is thinking when she says 'Yes' the second time.

4. At the end Miss Bell says 'No.' How is she feeling and how will she sound?

Excerpt shown:
Milly: Miss! Miss!
Miss Bell: Yes, Milly. What is it?
Milly: You know when I've measured out my ingredients and mixed them into dough?
Miss Bell: Yes.
Milly: And when I've rolled the dough flat with a rolling pin?
Miss Bell: Yes.
Milly: And when I've cut the dough into the shape of a gingerbread man and cooked him? Can I bite his head off?
Miss Bell: No.

Tricky Biscuits
Skill: Inferring characters' feelings for reading aloud with expression

About the Play

Reading Level
This play is suitable for children reading at approximately National Curriculum Level 2C, or 5–14 Level B.

Synopsis
Tricky Biscuits is a humorous play set in a school. It is written in natural language with a simple layout.

Miss Bell, the teacher, and a group of five children in her class are making gingerbread biscuits for the parents' evening that is taking place that night. However, instead of making them in the traditional shape of gingerbread men, Miss Bell asks the children to cut their dough into a shape that has something to do with their mum or dad, for example their work or their hobbies. The children get to work, though all Milly seems to want to do is eat them! When the biscuits are cooked, Miss Bell and the children look at each shape and try to guess what it is and what connection it has to the child's mum or dad. It seems like an easy enough task, but the children have been very imaginative and it's not always clear what the biscuits are supposed to be!

Characters
There are six characters in the play. Each of the characters also appears in the other two plays for Year 3 (P4), *Christmas Catastrophe* and *Farm Frights*.
- Miss Bell (teacher): Not very good at guessing what the biscuits mean.
- Milly (pupil): Tries to be funny and interrupts a lot.
- Katie (pupil): Gives clever answers.
- Akbar (pupil): Finishes the play with the funniest joke!
- William (pupil): Calm and sensible.
- Josh (pupil): Keen to be liked by his teacher.

Links with Whole-class Work
This play has been selected to enable children to make informed contributions to whole-class sessions. For example:
- Children could present extracts from the play, which they have read in guided reading, to the rest of the class.
- They could discuss the way we build a picture of each character through the things that they say or do.

- They could compare the presentation of each character in the three plays *Tricky Biscuits*, *Christmas Catastrophe* and *Farm Frights*.
- They could compare play scripts and prose, focusing on how setting and characters are presented. For example, in stories, the author may describe the character, whereas, in plays, the actors have to show what characters are like by the way they say their lines.
- They could perform the play for a wider audience. (See pages 14 and 15 for detailed guidance on staging the play.)

Other Navigator Plays for Year 3

- ***Christmas Catastrophe* by Bob Wilson**
Miss Bell's class are getting the school hall ready for Christmas, but is Milly really being helpful?
- ***Farm Frights* by Bob Wilson**
It's the first day of their farm holiday and Miss Bell's class need to fetch a bucket of water. But everyone's afraid of something…

Tricky Biscuits

Genre: Familiar setting; play
Author: Bob Wilson
Illustrator: Garry Parsons

Key Teaching Objectives

Lesson 1
Y3 Strand 1: 4 Develop and use specific vocabulary (e.g. play-related words and phrases)
Y3 Strand 7: 1 Identify the main points of sections of text
Y3 Strand 7: 2 Infer characters' feelings in fiction and consequences in logical explanations
Y3 Strand 7: 3 Identify how different texts are organised (e.g. recognise the key differences between prose and play script)
Y3 Strand 8: 2 Empathise with characters

At a Glance

Lesson 1: Focus on Features of Play Scripts
Lesson 2: Focus on Reading Aloud with Expression

In this funny play, Miss Bell and a group of five children in her class are making gingerbread biscuits for parents' evening. The children make the biscuits into shapes that have something to do with their mum or dad, but all Milly wants to do is eat them!

The familiar setting of a school classroom will allow children to bring their own experience of being at school to the play. They will be able to empathise with the characters who are much like themselves and, using the dialogue, infer characters' feelings from what they say. In turn, this will enable them to develop the skill of reading aloud with expression as they take on specific roles.

The play format provides the opportunity to compare prose and play script, identifying the key features of play scripts.

In talking about the play, children will be able to develop and use, in context, specific play-related vocabulary.

Lesson 1

Think
Pages 2–3

Read the title of the play to the children and ask them to flick through some of the pages looking at the text layout and illustrations. Ask the children what sort of text they think this is (*i.e. a play script*). Explain that this play is set in a school. Look at pages 2 and 3 together and discuss who the characters are.

Read and Respond
Pages 5–11

To establish that the children have understood the plot and the characters, ask them to contribute to identifying key points.

> The following questions can be used as prompts:
> - What does Milly like best? *Eating the biscuits!*
> - What does Miss Bell say to Milly? What does this tell you about Milly? *Miss Bell tells Milly not to be silly. This tells us that Milly is inclined to be silly.*
> - What does Miss Bell tell the group they are going to do? *They are going to make shaped biscuits for the parents' evening.*
> - What do the children do when the biscuits are cooked? *They guess what their friends have made.*

Going Deeper
Ask the children to give their initial impressions of the characters. Ensure the children scan the text for evidence.
- How do the children in the play feel about making biscuits? *Enthusiastic, excited.*
- Who is the most serious child? *Josh.*
- Who is the 'joker' among the children? *Milly.*

Challenge
Allocate parts to the children. Ask them to read the text, focusing on the part, or 'role', they have been allocated. Ask them how they can tell which is their part in the text. (*The name of the character is in bold before each speech.*)

 Focus on: Features of Play Scripts • Pages 5–6

Reflect

Discuss with the children key differences between prose and play script. Ask the children which character they would most like to play. Encourage them to give reasons for their answers, using evidence from the text.

Challenge
Discuss the children's opinions of Milly. How do they think she will cope with the task that Miss Bell has asked them to do?

Follow-up
PCM 1 Comprehension.
Challenge The children could think of adverbs to describe how Milly and Miss Bell say their speeches on page 8.

Lesson 2

Think
Ask the children to summarise what has happened in the play so far. Write some phrases from the text onto a flipchart: e.g. *What next?/I know, Miss!* Ask the children to read them aloud and discuss how the punctuation helps them decide how the phrases should sound.

Read and Respond
Pages 12–19

To establish that the children have understood the plot and the characters, ask them to contribute to identifying key points.

> The following questions can be used as prompts:
> - Why does Josh shape his biscuit like an owl? *Because his mum is a teacher. Owls and teachers are wise.*
> - How many biscuits did Milly make? Why? *Two – a top hat and a rabbit because her dad's hobby is magic.*
> - How did Milly make the rabbit disappear? *She ate it!*
> - What shape was Katie's biscuit? Why? *Her biscuit was in the shape of a tap because her mum is learning how to tap dance.*
> - What was funny about Akbar's biscuit? *It was in the shape of a circle because his father is a biscuit baker.*

Going Deeper
Read the play aloud in character parts. Remind the children to think about what the character is saying and to use the punctuation to help them read with pace and expression. Remind them also to come in quickly and maintain the pace.

Challenge
Look at Josh's last speech on page 13. Ask the children what they think the bracketed text – *(to Milly)* – is. Guide them to see that it is a 'stage direction' and should not be said aloud. What might Josh do to indicate that he is speaking to Milly?

Focus on: Reading Aloud with Expression
- Pages 13, 15

Reflect
Ask the children for their personal responses to the play. Encourage them to give reasons for their preferences.
- Did they like the play?
- Did they enjoy reading it aloud?
- Which character did they like best?

Challenge
Discuss the ending and elicit from the children what was funny about it. How do they think the characters might have said "Biscuits!" at the end? *They might have shouted it while laughing.*

Follow-up
PCM 2 Writing.
Challenge The children could add bracketed stage directions to their new scene to indicate how the words should be said.

Key Teaching Objectives
Lesson 2

Y3 Strand 1: 1 Choose and prepare poems or stories [plays] for performance, identifying appropriate expression, tone, volume and use of voices and other sounds

Y3 Strand 4: 2 Use some drama strategies to explore stories or issues

Y3 Strand 7: 1 Identify the main points of sections of text

Y3 Strand 7: 2 Infer characters' feelings in fiction and consequences in logical explanations

Y3 Strand 8: 1 Share and compare reasons for reading preferences

Y3 Strand 9: 1 Make decisions about form and purpose

Further writing
Children can write brief character descriptions and/or a summary of the play.

Focus on: Features of Play Scripts • Pages 5–6   (Lesson 1)

Page 5

Ask the children to look at the first two lines of text on page 5. What do they notice about how they are laid out? Lead them to describe how the text is in two columns, with the words on the left in bold type and the words on right in normal type.

- What do the words in bold indicate? *The name of the character who is speaking.*
- What are the words on the right? *They are the actual words that the character is speaking.*

Ask the children to read Miss Bell's first speech aloud. Ensure that they understand that the name of the character in bold is not read aloud, only the words on the right.

Write the sentence: *Miss Bell said, "Today we're going to make gingerbread biscuits."* Ask the children to read it. Talk about how, in prose, the speaker's name *is* read, and the actual words are placed within speech marks, whereas, in a play script, the speaker's name is *not* read, and there are no speech marks.

Challenge

> Ask the children why it is not necessary, when reading a play script aloud, to read the speaker's name. *Because we can see and hear who is speaking.*

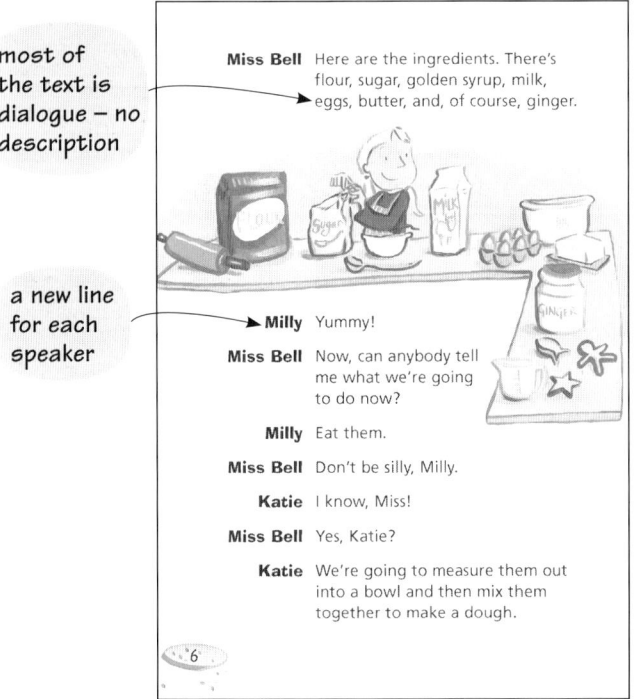

Page 6

Discuss how a play script is made up of dialogue with no description. The speech itself needs to include any description necessary.

Look at Miss Bell's first speech on page 6. What description does it include? *It describes (lists) the ingredients that are on the table.* Ask the children how this might have been described in prose. *For example, 'Miss Bell showed the children the ingredients. On the table, there was flour, sugar, golden syrup, milk, eggs, butter and, of course, ginger.'*

Having looked at some of the differences between prose dialogue and play script dialogue, discuss one of the similarities. Ask the children how a new speaker is indicated in a play script. *A new line is created for each speaker.* Is this the same for dialogue in prose? *Yes.*

Challenge

> Ask the children to try and tell the story on page 6 of the play script as prose.

◀ Turn back to **Reflect** on page 8

Focus on: Reading Aloud with Expression (Lesson 2)
• Pages 13, 15

Page 13
Ask the children to look at William's speech at the top of page 13.
- How do they think William is feeling? How might the reader say this speech? *He is confused. Might be said in a puzzled, questioning way.*
- Discuss the importance of taking into account the meaning of words and punctuation when reading aloud.

Look at other speeches on the page and ask the children how they might be said and why. For example:
- "Why is a teacher like an owl?" *Miss Bell shows that she's interested by asking a 'why' question. Will have a questioning tone.*
- "I thought she would." *Josh knew Miss Bell would be pleased and he's being smug.*

Ask the children what the words in brackets mean in Josh's last speech. *They are stage directions indicating that Josh is directing this speech to Milly.* Discuss how stage directions tell the actor how to act and are *not* read aloud.

Challenge
Ask the children to read some of the speeches on page 13 with and without the punctuation. This will demonstrate its importance.

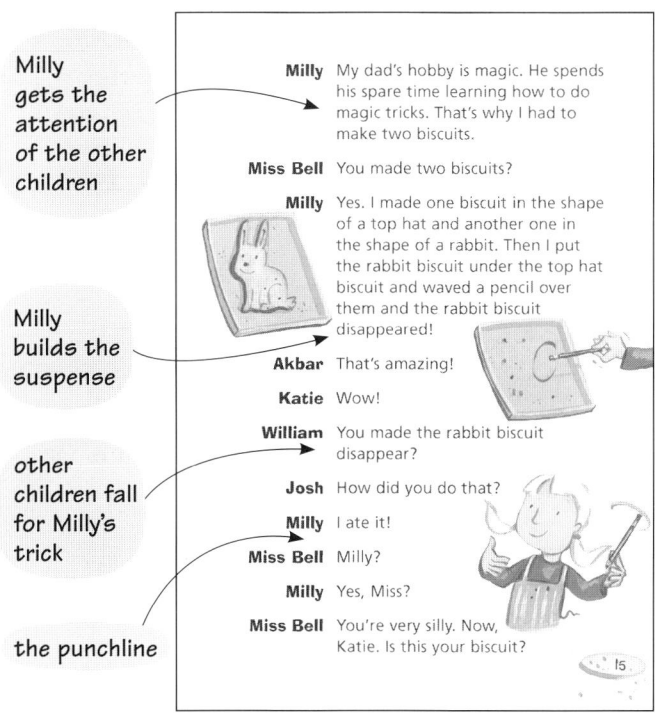

Page 15
Read Milly's first speech on page 15 aloud. Ensure that the last sentence is said with emphases on the words "That's" and "two". Ask the children why you emphasised those words. Guide them to see that Milly is boasting.

Ask the children to look at Milly's second speech and to tell you how they think it should be read. *Milly is describing what she did, but she takes her time about it, building up the suspense. The reader could start slowly and quietly, getting faster and louder.*

Now look at William's line.
- What kind of sentence is it? *Question.* How can they tell? *There is a question mark at the end.*
- How should it be said? *In an amazed, questioning way.*

Ask one of the children to read Milly's line "I ate it!" with appropriate expression. Ask the other children to comment.

Challenge
Ask the children to explain the trick Milly has played.

Turn back to **Reflect** on page 9

Name: _____ **Date:** _____

Re-read page 8 of *Tricky Biscuits*.

Then answer the questions on another piece of paper.

❶ At the beginning Milly says "Miss! Miss!". How is she feeling? How will she sound?

❷ Milly asks three questions in a row. How do you think she will sound each time?

❸ Miss Bell says 'Yes' twice. Will she sound the same each time? Write what you think she is thinking when she says 'Yes' the second time.

❹ At the end Miss Bell says 'No.' How is she feeling and how will she sound?

Milly	Miss! Miss!
Miss Bell	Yes, Milly. What is it?
Milly	You know when I've measured out my ingredients and mixed them up into dough?
Miss Bell	Yes.
Milly	And when I've rolled the dough flat with a rolling pin?
Miss Bell	Yes.
Milly	And when I've cut the dough into the shape of a gingerbread man and cooked him? Can I bite his head off?
Miss Bell	No.

PCM 1

Tricky Biscuits
Skill: Inferring characters' feelings for reading aloud with expression

Name: _____ **Date:** _____

Look again at the part of the play where Miss Bell is trying to guess what William has made (page 11).

What kind of biscuit would you make?

Write a new page for the play where you show Miss Bell your biscuit and tell her what it is.

Miss Bell	Let's have a look at the shapes you've made.
Me	Look Miss, you'll never guess what I've made!
Miss Bell	_____
Me	_____
Miss Bell	_____

Tricky Biscuits
Skill: Writing in play script format using reading as a model

Now Stage the Play

These notes are designed to suggest ways in which the script may be brought to life in performance, rather than just read as a text. How you use them will obviously depend on whether you are staging the play to be performed in front of a wider audience, or whether you intend the children to use the "Ready, steady, act!" notes from their play scripts to develop a performance by themselves, maybe in guided reading sessions.

Suggestions have been given for props, costumes and production techniques, but many are optional. There is still great value in performing the play without too much practical effort however limited your resources may be.

What you will need
- empty food containers for ingredients
- mixing bowls and spoons
- rolling pin
- six biscuits shaped as a square, a bird, a top hat, a rabbit, a tap and a circle. They could be made from paper or card
- a baking tray
- aprons
- suitable costume for Miss Bell.

Choosing the parts
How you cast the play will depend on whether you are expecting the children to learn lines or to read the play while acting. You may want to give parts with more lines to children who will cope better.

The main acting challenge in *Tricky Biscuits* is Miss Bell. The actor playing her will need to convey authority and therefore have confidence. To distinguish her physically from the pupils, the part might also be played by a taller child. However, a suitable costume and accessories (e.g. dress, glasses, necklace) will adequately portray the character as an adult.

You may wish to 'audition' the children:
- Ask them to read a few lines of the play and see who is best.
- Ask them to show you some frozen facial expressions of a character.

There are only six parts in this play. If you wish to include the rest of the class you could:
- add them as non-speaking classmates
- have a small group of theatre critics
- have a group responsible for costumes and props
- ask a group or individual to direct the play
- ask a group to design and publish a programme.

Characters
Explain to the children that *becoming* a character can teach us a great deal more about that character than just reading the part aloud.
- Develop a tableau (frozen picture) of the characters on pages 4 and 5 of the play. What do their positioning and body language tell us about them?
- Ask the children to say a familiar rhyme in the style of Miss Bell and then Milly.

Setting the scene
The action takes place in a classroom environment. Talk with the children about how they feel in class when the teacher announces that they are to have an unusual lesson such as cooking.
- How does the mood of the class alter? Ask them to show you.
- What might the children say to one another or to the teacher? Take suggestions.

Speaking and Moving

Speaking
Look at the cast list on pages 2 and 3 and ask the children what they know about the characters.
- How will Miss Bell's speech differ from that of the children?
- Will the children all speak in the same way or will some of them be cheerful or whining or cheeky?

Encourage the children to use their voices to show the different personalities of the actors and the changing mood of Miss Bell.
- On page 18, Akbar probably becomes quite frustrated at Miss Bell's attempts to guess. He says "No" five times. How should they differ?
- On page 15, Milly is quite cheeky when she says she ate the rabbit biscuit. How will Miss Bell sound when she responds?

At several points in the script the children call out together like a chorus, saying, "Hooray!" and "Biscuits!" This is worth practising as ensemble speaking can be messy.

Moving

As the play takes place in a classroom, the whole cast remains on stage throughout. This is a great opportunity for teaching the actors to 'stay in character'. Discuss with the children how they can show the audience that they are still acting even though it is not their turn to speak.

- Ask them to mime making biscuits in the background.
- Discuss what else might be happening. Maybe some children are being naughty.

It is important that they learn not to detract from the main action.

Evaluating the Performance

Drama Objectives	Teachers	Pupils
Present events and characters through dialogue to engage the interest of an audience	Were the voices audible and interesting? Did the children stay in character?	Did the cast feel that the audience was entertained?
Use some drama strategies to explore stories or issues	**Group discussion:** What do the children understand about teacher/pupil relationships?	Is it all right to have fun with teachers by being a little cheeky?
Identify and discuss qualities of others' performances, including gesture, action and costume	Question and answer session to find out the opinions of the actors and the audience.	Ask audience members to write reviews of the play.

Further Ideas

- Write and then perform a scene for the part in the play where the biscuits are in the oven.
- Improvise a scene where the children are actually making the biscuits.
- Of course, you may wish to actually *make* some biscuits!

Rigby
Halley Court, Jordan Hill, Oxford, OX2 8EJ
Rigby is an imprint of Pearson Education Limited, a company incorporated in England and Wales, having its registered office at Edinburgh Gate, Harlow, Essex, CM20 2JE.
Registered company number: 872828

www.rigbyed.co.uk

Rigby is a registered trademark of Reed Elsevier, Inc, licensed to Pearson Education Limited

© Jean Kendall and Pearson Education Ltd, 2008

First published 2008

All rights reserved. The material in this publication is copyright. Pupil sheets may be freely photocopied for classroom use in the purchasing institution. However, this material is copyright and under no circumstances may copies be offered for sale. If you wish to use the material in any way other than that specified you must apply in writing to the publishers.

Tricky Biscuits Teaching Notes   ISBN 978 0 433011 78 1
Tricky Biscuits 6 pack with Teaching Notes   ISBN 978 0 433011 03 3

12 11 10 09 08
10 9 8 7 6 5 4 3 2 1

Series Editors for original version: Chris Buckton, Jean Kendall and Alison Price
Original Teaching Notes written by Jean Kendall
This version written by Gina Nuttall with Lesley Ford, Mike Levy and Alison MacDonald
National Curriculum levelling by Suzanne Baker and Shirley Bickler
Illustrated by Garry Parsons
Logo artwork by Max Ellis
Typeset by Planman Technologies, India
Printed and bound in the UK by Ashford Colour Press